Copyright 2013 Keir McLaren
All Rights Reserved

Available from amazon.com
and other online stores

Henry Kids Picture Books

Available From Amazon.com and other online stores.

Henry Meets a Tree-Legged Dog

Henry Saves Nana's Garden

Henry Visits The World's Silliest Zoo

ABSTRACT

Abstract #1

Abstract #2

Bad Dream

Abstract: Paper 53 #1

Abstract #17

ART

Abstract: Paper 53 #2

Abstract #57

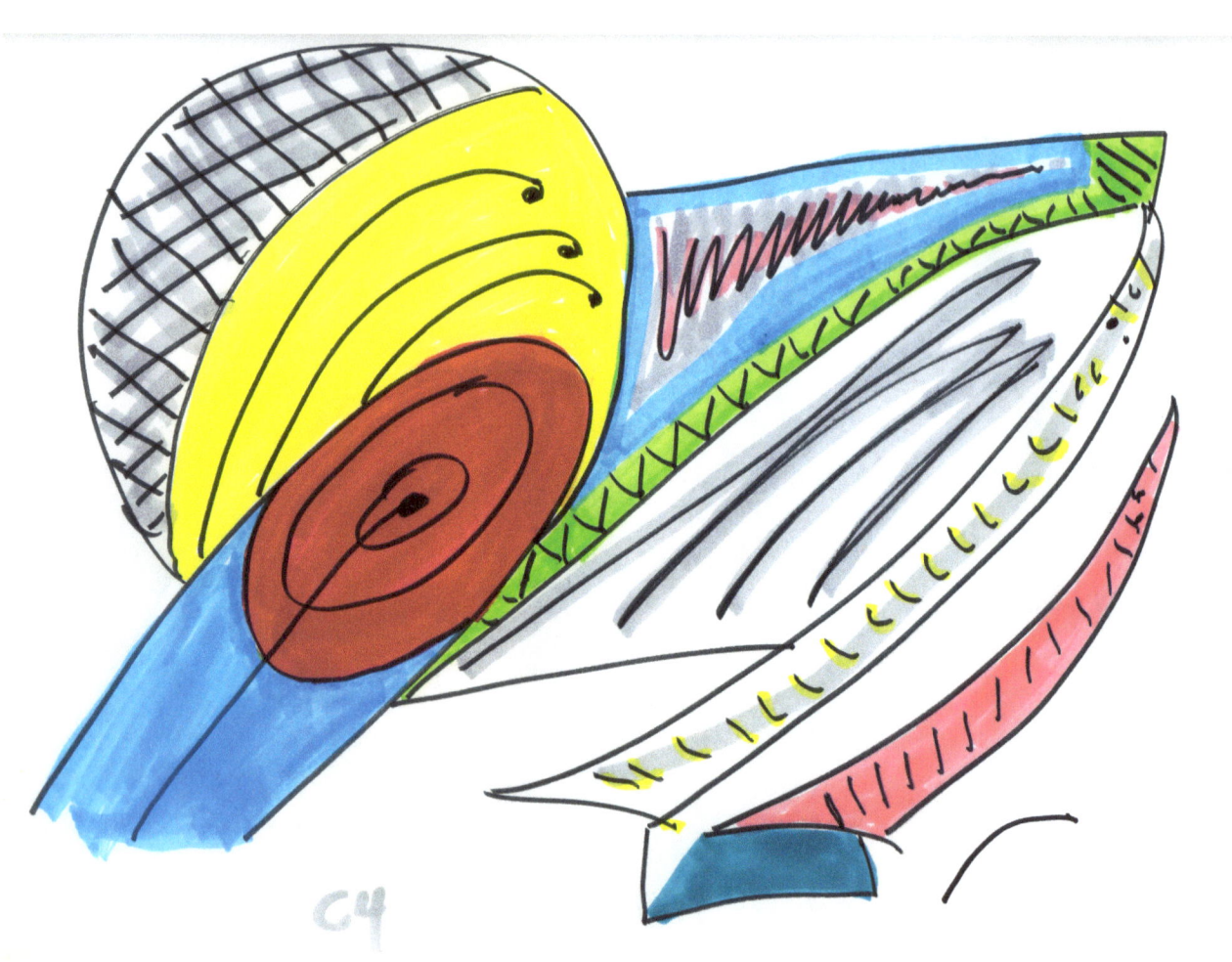

C4

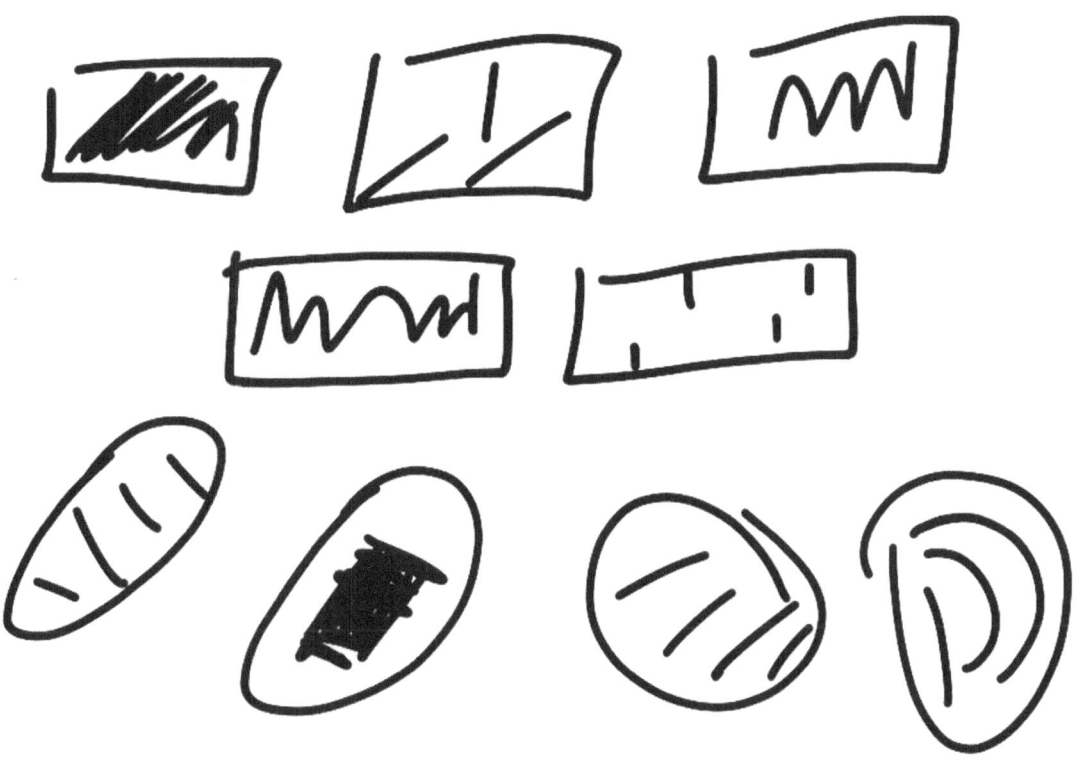

Abstract: Paper 53 #3

Abstract #42

fuc'nt

Summer

Connections

Mexico City #1

Mexico City #2

Mexico City #3

Abstract 42

Abstract 31

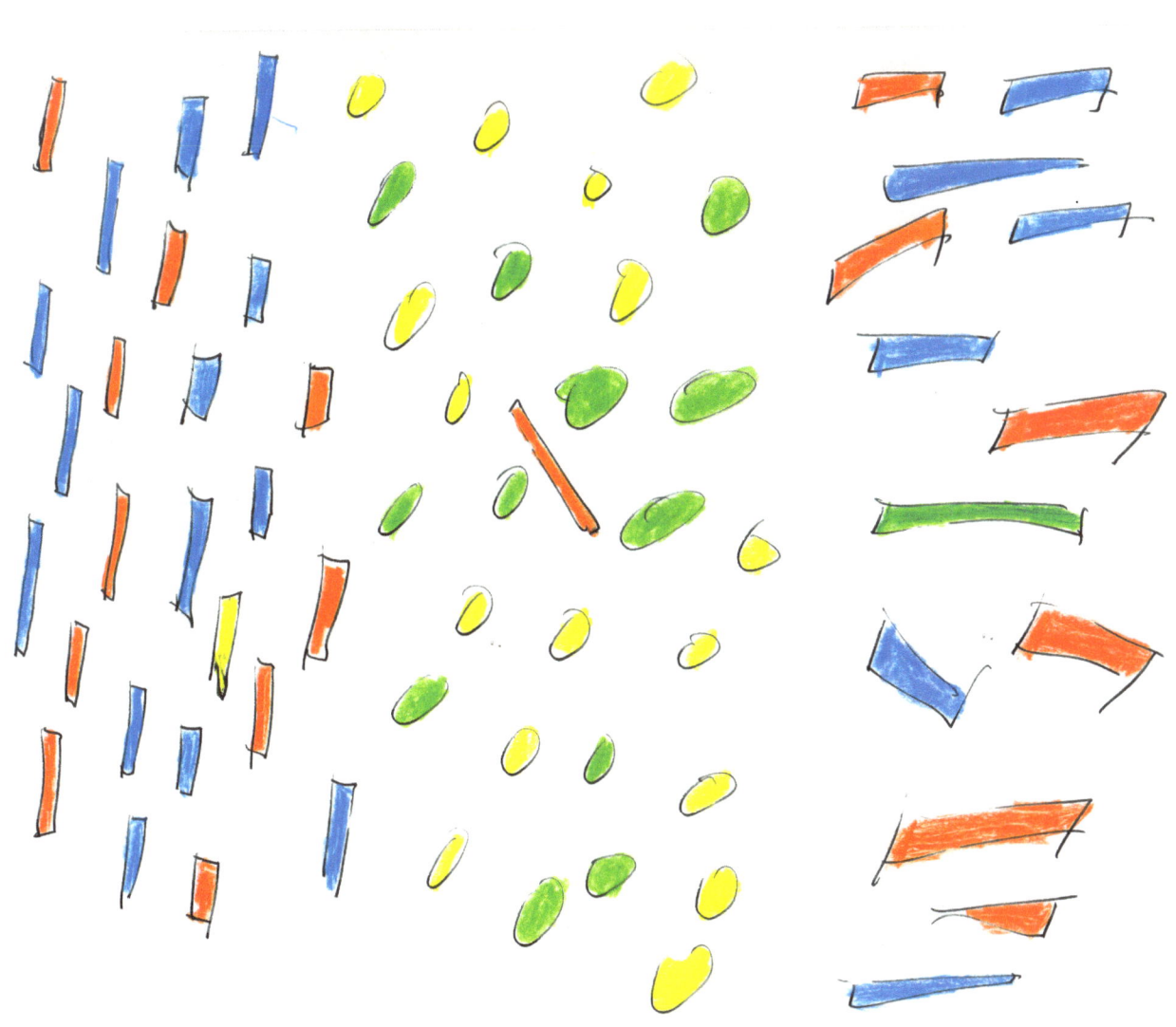

Abstract #20

Abstract #17

GROSZ STYLE

George Grosz (July 26, 1893 – July 6, 1959) was a German artist known especially for his caricatural drawings of decadent Berlin life in the 1920s.

Power

Never Enough

After The Flag Waving's Over

The Final Super Size

Berlin Beer

At Your Service

Steamfitter

Dee

Wall Street Guy

Smoker's Dream

Man #7

People, Places & Esoterica

Boy

William Lloyd Garrison
(December 12, 1805 – May 24, 1879)

President Obama

Deadbeat Dad

LACK OF IDEALS = CONFORMITY……………………

Paris Street #1

Paris Street # 2

Albert Camus

Cuba

We decide who you are.
We decide what you think.
We decide who decides.

Isms

Cat Boot

Man #7: Paper 53

Man #12: paper 53

Hippie

Kells Jesus

HE WHO LAUGHS
HAS NOT YET
HEARD THE
BAD NEWS!

BERTOLT BRECHT

Bertolt Brecht

Studious

"Artists are here to disturb the peace."
James Baldwin: 1924-1987

Teresa -A Rose Among The Thorns

Rembrandt van Rijn

Good Look'in

Monk, Ai Weiwei & Mustafa Abdul Jalil

1930

Man #11

Poly Styrene